JOKES FOR KIDS

Funny Laugh-out-Loud Jokes and One-Liners for Children and Young Adults to Help Build Their Vocabulary

Written by: Nina Riddle

Jokes for Kids: Funny Laugh-out-Loud Jokes and One-Liners for Children and Young Adults to Help Build Their Vocabulary

Published in the United States of America.

Q R F 9 2 8 4 2 1

JOKES FOR KIDS

What do horses put on their tuna sandwiches? *Hayonnaise*.

What did the jeans say to the t-shirt when their team was losing badly? *"We should give up, it's overalls."*

What time in the morning does the bakery open? *Just after bunrise.*

What do deaf people drink on a hot day? *Hearingade*.

Why don't pandas get invited on canoe trips? *Instead of bringing paddles they bring pandamonium.*

Why don't chimpanzees make very good police officers? *They're no good at tailing people.*

Why didn’t the fog show up for work? *He was feeling under the weather.*

What did the old lady name her pet oyster? *Pearl.*

How do you get a hamburger to admit to a crime? *You grill it until it confesses.*

What do fish listen to on the internet? *Codcasts.*

Where do polar bears keep their money? *Snow banks.*

What do you call a moldy old jack-o'-lantern? *A dumpkin.*

Why are cows good at basketball? *Because they know how to jump over the mooooooooon.*

Why was the cricket player kicked off the team? *After they lost the big game he went batty.*

What did the butter knife say to the steak knife? *You're looking sharp.*

Why aren't bananas good at hockey? *They keep slipping on the ice.*

Why do chickens make great rock stars?
They’ve been using drumsticks all their lives.

How do you make Indian food run faster?
Hurry powder.

Why did the oil pipeline join the army? *He wanted to be a drill sergeant.*

What was the figure skater's favorite color?
Pink rink.

Why are photographers great at laser tag?
They like to shoot things.

What's the secret to daffodil cupcakes?
Baking flower.

Why don't mosquitos like baseball? *They feel uncomfortable when the players hit a fly ball.*

Why did the snake lose the election? *His favorite game was Follow the Leader.*

What do cowboys eat for breakfast? *Western omelets.*

Why did the server quit his job? *He was tired of being a barftender.*

What color did the dog paint his house? *Bark green.*

Why don't cars make good politicians? *Because they're wheely bad at public speaking.*

What do you call a yam in a bad mood? *A grumpy potato.*

Why don't sand monsters make good clowns? *Their sense of humor is too dry.*

Where do cars and trucks visit when they travel to northern Europe? *Tireland.*

Why is lettuce good at accounting? *It has real head for it.*

Why did the bunny flunk his geometry course? *He harely showed up.*

Why was chocolate late for work? *He had trouble pudding on his tie.*

What do you call it when everyone takes off their socks and stinks up the room? *A feet wave.*

Why did the foot go a date with the fist? *He was very handsome.*

Why do military bases have lots of security cameras? *They're afraid of tank robbers.*

Why didn’t the duck go skydiving? *She was too chicken.*

What do baby scallywags wear on their feet? *Pirate booties.*

How does a cloud get from the suburbs to downtown in 15 minutes? *She hails a cab.*

Why are some computers bad at chess? *They don't have the memory for it.*

Which country had never won an Olympic medal in track and field? *Sprain*.

What do you call an accident that happens after someone is scared by a loud noise? *A thunder blunder.*

Where do giant worms go on vacation? *The Big Apple.*

What did the peanut farmer say to his delivery driver when he wouldn't stop humming? *"Cut it out, you're driving me nuts."*

What time of day do geese settle their arguments? *High loon.*

Why did the broom get fired? *He was sweeping on the job.*

Who delivers babies to the gods that live in the sky? *The thunderstork.*

Why did the snowman quit his job at the library and become a police officer? *He wanted to solve cold cases not book cases.*

What do you call a bunch of old ladies carrying rolled-up newspapers. *A SWAT team.*

Why don't the wives of basketball players wear earrings? *They're tired of all the hoops.*

Why do feet make great doctors? *They have magical heeling powers.*

How don't bakers use Microsoft Excel? *It doesn't have the breadsheet features they're looking for.*

Why did the car run into the truck? *He didn't eat his brakefast.*

What’s a snake’s favorite course in school? *Hissssstory.*

What sort of computers do babies use? *Naptops.*

What do gardeners eat after going to the gym to help build muscle? *Flower bars.*

Why did the cell phone move her wedding date? *She couldn't get reception.*

Why can't shoes use computers? *They don't know how to boot them.*

Why did the flashlight fail her final exam? *She wasn't bright enough.*

How was the birthday cake feeling when the girl blew out the candles? *It was feeling delighted.*

What do nightstands order when they go out for dinner? *Lamp chops.*

Where do Blu-Ray players take their families on vacation? *To exotic and remote locations.*

Why does everyone say a box can't come up with good ideas? *His ideas are always corrugated or too thin.*

Where do speedy people throw their garbage? *In the dash can.*

Why did racecar driver put a big bet on himself to win the Indy 500? *He was carfident he would win.*

Why did the brain surgeon get a part time job at the phone company? *He was a good operator.*

Why don't thermometers go to college? *They've already multiple degrees.*

What do you call a dog that swims long distance races in the Olympics? *A lap dog.*

What sort of emails do basketball players like to get? *Dunk mail.*

Why don't birds use computers? *They don't like windows.*

Why did the restaurant fire its website? *It wasn't a good server.*

What do you call a stinky statue? *Fart art.*

Why was father upset with mother? *She was being mum about where she wanted to go for dinner.*

What do you call those annoying pieces of lint that stick to knitted garments? *Scarf barf.*

Why was the maple leaf rushed to the hospital? *He had a bad fall.*

What did the fruit salad say when her friend kept talking about her Caribbean vacation? *"Jamaican me wanna cuba guatamelon."*

Why the cockroach leave the party early? *She didn't want to be a pest.*

What was the gunslinger's favorite book when he was young? *Green Eggs and Blam.*

What do pancakes do when they don't like what's on TV? *They flip the channel.*

Why couldn't the gypsy see the future? *She was too present-minded.*

Why didn't the rodent like working indoors? *He was a field mouse.*

What do you call a depressed cruise liner? *A woe boat.*

What did the painting name his kid? *Art.*

What country sells the most winter jackets? *Chile.*

What do wizards put on their pizza instead of fresh basil? *Sage.*

What did the jet fighter give the spaceshuttle when he asked her to marry him? *An engagement wing.*

Why did the computer mouse get sent to bed without desert? *He was a cursor.*

Why did the roast turkey say to the taxi driver? *"Thanksgiving me a lift."*

When eggs go to the beach who helps them build a sand castle? *Sea shells.*

What color were the pillows in the airplane? *Flight blue.*

Who organized the math teacher's bachelor party? *The test man.*

Why do guinea pigs buy their groceries? *Hamsterdam.*

What do stars produce on their days off? *Funshine.*

What do swamp monsters leave at the end of a rainbow? *A pot of mold.*

Which country has the nicest dinnerware? *The United Plates.*

Why did the mechanic get a virus on his computer. *He turned off his tirewall.*

Why don't young children make good tennis players? *They don't like squash.*

How does a muskrat ask a beaver on a date? He says, *"Do you want to gopher coffee?"*

What did the pirate give out for Halloween? *A-sworded candy.*

What do you call a woman's closet that's filled with sneakers. *A lair of shoes.*

Which Sesame Street character spends all his time on the internet? *Cookie Monster.*

What do karate fighters wear under their clothes? *Boxer shorts.*

What's a duck's favorite snack? *Cheese and quackers.*

What do you call an elf that works at the library? *A book sh-elf.*

What do you call alligator who works for the police department? *An investigator.*

What do you call a big raindrop? *A maindrop.*

Where was the dolphin prince born? *Wales.*

Why don't anchovies shake hands after they lose a game? *They're too salty.*

Why did the puddle lose his job as a car salesman? *He was all dried up.*

What is a dog's favorite instrument? *Wag pipes.*

Why was the bird angry with his hair stylist? *He didn't want to be a bald eagle.*

Why do elf feet make great sandwich toppings? *They taste like toematoes.*

What do you call a hamburger with two carrots sticking out of it? *Horned beef.*

What did the spice rack say to cupboard when a chipmunk ran through the kitchen? *"I don't have thyme for this."*

Why wasn't the princess blessed on her naming day? *Instead of a fairy godmother she had a lazy godmother.*

Why do farm dogs buy new cars? *They're bad at leashing them.*

Which sea creature makes the best tuba player? *The blow fish.*

What did the skunk want for his birthday because all his friends had one? *A smell phone.*

Where do cyborgs like to hang out? *In cyber space.*

Why don't plumbers like to fix bathtubs? *The work is very draining.*

Why are cows good at killing vampires? *They've always got a steak handy.*

When is the best time of day to eat candy? *Sour hour.*

Why are toilets bad at poker? *Because when they get a good hand theirs faces are flushed.*

Which country is always trying to keep up with the latest fashion trends? *Fadagascar.*

Why didn't the bullfighter want to get in the ring with the horse? *He was a coward.*

What do teachers eat after doing arts and crafts? *Tapefruit.*

What do you call a mountain that never explodes? *A volcanot.*

What do you call a giant ape that hits a gong? *Donkey Bong*.

What do you call an annoying person related to you by marriage? *A bother-in-law.*

Which country are most chess champions from? *The Check Republic.*

Why didn't the saxophone get a part in the school play? *He blew his audition.*

Why didn't the blind man like to visit California? *He could never find Lost Angeles.*

Why was the painting denied a bank loan? *It was overdrawn.*

What do call a cloud that's out of breath? *Winded.*

Why did the anteater's program crash? *It had too many bugs.*

Why was the gauntlet so depressed? *He was in glove with a sock but she shooed him away.*

Where do rats like to go on vacation? *Miceland.*

Which country always helps their friends when they move? *Packistan.*

Which people make the best sprinters? *Russians.*

Why didn't the ravine like the short film? *It was too depressing.*

How do snarky football players like their eggs? *Over easy.*

What is a tiger shark's favorite kind of sandwich? *Peanut butter and jellyfish.*

Where do hard drives hang their clothes? *In a storage closet.*

Why did the head cook fire his new sous chef? *He was pot-headed.*

Why did Alice bring a net and a jar to school? *She didn't want to lose the spelling bee.*

Why did the brain surgeon ask his boss for a new computer? *It had a better operating system.*

Which is the saddest spider? *The black widow.*

Where do internet ogres live? *In the blog.*

Why didn't the two butchers get along? *There was a lot of beef between them.*

Why couldn't the fish log into his email? *He forgot his bassword.*

What do you call a hippopotamus in a bad mood? *Hangry.*

What do you call a river that gets warmer every day and tumbles off a cliff? *A hotterfall.*

Why do people love FedEx? *They get your package delivered freight away.*

What did the lemon send back his fajitas? *The restaurant was out of sour cream.*

Why don't turtles make good wizards? *They're always late.*

Why do cowboys have long hair? *Because they like to tie it back in a ponytail.*

Why are ghosts not allowed into comedy clubs? *They always boo the comedians.*

What should you do if you see an envelope on fire? *Stamp it out.*

Why do street signs make good stock traders? *They know how to corner the market.*

What did the cob of corn ask Santa for? *World peas.*

What dog gets along the best with cows? *A bulldog.*

What did the river say to the engineer? *"Want to play bridge?"*

What do you call someone who's allergic to French fries? *A notato.*

Which country do dogs avoid visiting because it's run by cats? *Fleegypt.*

What did the tomato say to the cucumber? *"Lettuce get out here before we end up in the chopper."*

What kind of bread do lemons eat? *Sourdough.*

Why do the police do when they arrest a cup of coffee with a picture of a fish on it? *They take its mug shot then throw it in the drink.*

Why didn't the ghost come to the dance? *Because he had no-body to go with him.*

What do you call a 40-year-old knight in shining armor? *Middle-aged.*

How did the ball of yarn get a job at the bank? *She pulled some strings.*

Why was the palm tree sent to the Arkham asylum? *He was a real coconut.*

How do librarians get books to walk themselves to the front desk? *They page them.*

Where country did the frog win a vacation to? *Flyland.*

Why does bread make you fat? *Because if you eat too much you'll loaf around all day.*

What do gymnasts wear instead of makeup? *Flipstick.*

What do pastry squirrels eat for dinner? *Doughnuts.*

What do you call a funnel cloud that quickly vanishes? *A boringnado.*

Where do fish sleep? *In tiny river beds.*

How do hornets send letters to their grandparents? *Bee-mail.*

What did the snapping turtles wear when he went to grandma's for dinner? *A turtleneck.*

What happens when two loaves of bread get married? *Someone gives a toast.*

Which movie won best picture at the 1973 fish Oscars? *The Codfather.*

What do wizards eat when they go to the beach? *Sandwitches.*

What do ghouls eat for Sunday dinner? *Ghost beef.*

Why aren't tennis players allowed in movie theaters? *They're always making a racket.*

What do rabbits use after they wash their head with shampoo? *Hare conditioner.*

What is flavor of yogurt does the common cold eat? *Fluberry.*

Which country has the nicest boulders? *Irock.*

What does the world's best Italian chef put on his spaghetti? *Masta sauce.*

How do people on vacation like their eggs? *Sunny side up.*

Why are pirate themed parties so expensive? *The parents always go overboard with the decorations.*

What did the suit salesman say to Albert Einstein after he tried on a tuxedo? *"You're looking smart."*

Why did the praying mantis get hit by the tennis ball? *He was too green.*

Why did the cloud make a bad king? *He didn't like to rain.*

What do clocks do when they don’t trust their doctor? *They get a second opinion.*

Why do lobsters make great judges? *They do well in claw school.*

Why were the grapes sent to bed early? They were starting to wine.

Why was the laundry sent down to the minor leagues? *He was all washed up.*

Why did the bird refuse to take his medicine? *He was tired of being a swallow.*

What do birds call the multicolored meteorological phenomenon that appears in the sky? *A cranebow.*

Why wasn’t the polygon invited to the beach? *He was a square.*

What do you call it when two cows are sitting in a squad car watching the farmer's house? *A steak out.*

What do trees wear when they go hiking? *Root boots.*

Why didn’t security let the metal door into the White House? *He didn’t pass the screening.*

Why don't snowmen like skateboards? *They prefer to ride their bicicles.*

Why don’t spoons like to go hiking? *They don’t like running into forks in the road.*

What was the dentist’s favorite ride at the amusement park? *The molar coaster.*

Why did the computer win the boxing match? *He had a lot of BAM.*

Why are farmers good at playing pool? *They're handy with a cue-cumber.*

What do you call it when tropical trees start swaying in the wind? *The palm before the storm.*

Which country has the most heavy metal music bands? *Bangladrum.*

Why do chairs make lousy baseball players? *They always get benched.*

What country is fun to visit because it can snow in the middle of summer? *The Weatherlands.*

Why don't email servers ever get hungry? *They eat a lot of spam.*

What is dad's favorite snack? *Popcorn.*

What's the best type of letter to get on a hot summer's day? *Fan mail.*

Why did the nectarine do well in school? *His teachers all thought he was a real peach.*

How do planets clean themselves? *They take a meteor shower.*

What type of fruit do people without hands like to eat? *Strawberries.*

What do squid do when they feel sick? *Visit the doctopus.*

Why do gold medal winners never delete their emails? *They have a big winbox.*

What did the hotdog tell the hamburger when he was getting too far ahead of her? *"Slow down and let me ketchup."*

Why do football players like a lot of cereal for breakfast? *Because they get to eat it from a super bowl.*

Why couldn't the computer get a job? *It was bad with applications.*

What did the apricot say to the prune? *“Want to go on a date?”*

Why did the annoying tree get cut down? *He was throwing too much shade.*

Why don’t trees keep their money in the bank? *They’ve already got a branch.*

What did the log cabin say after the tree told her she was beautiful? *"You're pretty wood-looking yourself."*

Why did the sled dog go on strike? *He was tired of being fed mushrooms.*

Aside from Paris, where do most women want to go on their honeymoon? *Romancia.*

Why did the gardener get married in his tool shed? *He didn't want anybody to eat his wedding rake.*

What do you call an angry skateboarder? *Rad-tempered.*

Why don’t omelets go to college? *They can’t pass their high school eggzams.*

What do mice say when they lose at checkers. *Rats!*

Why do painters make good gunslingers? *They're fast at drawing.*

What city do bulls and steers consider an exotic location? *Moscow.*

What was the secret ingredient that made the snowman's fajitas so tasty? *Chili pepper.*

Why do geologists love baseball? *It's played on a diamond.*

What did the bathroom say to the kitchen when the Titanic hit the iceberg? *"I had a sinking feeling that was going to happen."*

How does your body know when it's time to fight off an infection? *It gets a call on its white blood cell phone.*

Why did the spider sign up for high-speed internet? *She wanted to build a web page.*

Why did the painting get arrested? *Because he was framed.*

What's the secret to great airline food? *Just plane flour.*

Why was the computer conference a failure? *The speakers weren't very good.*

Why did the skeleton visit WebMD? *He couldn't stop coffin.*

Why wasn't the delivery truck allowed into the army corps of engineers? *He failed the stress test.*

What's the secret to snowman curry? *Nothing, it's just chicken and ice.*

Where do Swedish fish love to go on vacation? *Finland.*

How do put baby NASA scientist to sleep? *Sing her a song and rocket her back-and-forth.*

What does the alarm clock do before he drinks his coffee? *He reads the snooze paper.*

What kind of tree do you never want to watch a sad movie with? *A weeping willow.*

Who is the cloud's favorite super hero? *The Flash of Lighting.*

What do mummies like on their granola?
Tutmeg.

Why did the clown quit his job at the circus?
He broke his funny bone.

What kind of snake do mechanics keep as a pet? *Windshield vipers.*

How do get a squirrel to paint your ceiling?
Offer it some wallnuts.

What do you call it when it's raining one minute and sunny out the next? *Climate strange.*

What do you call bride who falls in a puddle of mud? *A wedding mess.*

What do ogres eat for lunch? *Club sandwiches.*

Which country always wins the gold medal in the 10 kilometer dash? *Ranada*

Why did the gorilla get detention? *He was monkeying around in class.*

Why did the princess stay out past her bedtime? *She was having a fun knight.*

What did the dog want for Easter to go along with his new suit and tie? *Rufflinks.*

What did the crab name her shell? *Sandy.*

Why did the keyboard break up with the pen? *She wasn't his type.*

What didn't the motorcycle want go to bed? *He wasn't tired.*

Why didn't the blanket go to jail? *He was found not quilty.*

Why do cats like computers? *They like to play with the mouse.*

Why do shoes bad at public speaking?
They've got nothing to talk aboot.

Why do villains make good story tellers?
They're good at plotting.

Why do birds like to sleep in fir trees? *It keeps them warm at night.*

Where does the pig do his summer reading?
In the hammock.

Why didn't the turkey cross the road? *He was a chicken.*

What type of dog did Albert Einstein have? *A black physics lab.*

What did the clam eat to get big and strong? *Muscles.*

What do indecisive people use to protect themselves from the rain? *An ummmmmmmmmmmbrella.*

Why don't clouds make good salespeople? *They don't like high pressure systems.*

Which country always makes a good deal in trade negotiations? *Fairaguay.*

What do frogs sit on at a restaurant? *Toad stools.*

Why are kitchens good at math? *They have a lot of counters.*

What do sports cars do on their day off? *Rewax.*

What did mustard say when ketchup asked her out on a date? *"I relish the idea of spending time with a hot dog like you."*

Why don't horses like spicy food? *It has too much of a kick.*

Why did the dog throw away her computer? *She didn't like the fleaboard.*

What do shiny pebbles want to be when they grow up? *Rock stars.*

What does a nose use to keep his pants up? *A smelt.*

What was the name of the scrawny knight who won the jousting tournament? *Sir Prise!!!*

What did the pastry chef tell his apprentice when the cookies started to burn? *"Butter get on that."*

What do untrustworthy women wear on their feet when they go to fancy parties? *Lie heels.*

Why didn't the android want any eggs for breakfast? *His brains were scrambled.*

What do you call an unattractive caterpillar? *Bugly.*

Why did the lumberjack leave before the opera was finished? *He was board.*

What animal is banned from every restaurant? *The ducked bill platypus.*

What do you call a restaurant that serves food infused with cocoa beans? *A bar of chocolate.*

How do satellite repairmen like their eggs? *Scrambled.*

Why don't baseball players ask for water when they go to a restaurant? *They've already got a pitcher.*

Why do grandfathers watch so much boxing? *They like to see people get clocked.*

What is the karate kid's favorite drink? *Fruit punch.*

Which country celebrates Halloween once a month? *Booganda.*

What did the police officer say to the snowman who was robbing a bank? *"Freeze! I've got hairdryer and I'm not afraid to use it."*

Why did the magnets get married so quickly? *They were attracted to each other.*

What did the fog say to the grass? *"I mist you."*

What did the yeti use to decorate his cupcakes? *Frosting.*

Where are doorbells manufactured? *The United Dingdom.*

Why is root beer fun at parades? *It makes a good float.*

What do call the chance looking out your window and seeing cows? *The leather forecast.*

Why did the dog bite the doctor? *He didn't want a cat scan.*

How do broken electronics like their eggs? *Fried.*

What do snowmen tell door-to-door salesmen when they don't want to buy anything? *"There's snowbody here, go away!"*

Why did the candle quit his telemarketing job? *He got burned out.*

Why did the bird call his parents and ask for money? *He was a bad budgier.*

Why did the fruit salad get kicked off the hockey team? *He lost his pear of skates.*

Why did the teacup complain to her travel agent? *Her honeymoon was too sweet.*

Why did the koala leave the zoo? *He couldn't bear it any longer.*

Where do rocket scientists eat their snacks? *On the lunch pad.*

What does dad buy to drink when he goes to the movies? *Soda pop.*

What do internet pirates do when they get a hole in their shoe? *They reboot.*

What do trains wear when they go jogging? *A tracksuit.*

What do skeletons order when they eat at a BBQ restaurant? *Spare ribs.*

Why can't you boil a chicken? *They're eggcelent swimmers.*

What's a swamp monster's favorite game?
Muck muck goose.

Why don't grapes work in an orphanage?
They get tired of raisin all those kids.

Why aren't oysters good at making friends?
When they meet new people their hands get clammy.

What did the shore say when the beach set her drink down on the coffee table? *"Put a coast under that."*

What do birds do when their Ikea furniture doesn't come with directions? *They wing it.*

Why did the octopus cancel his home phone? *He bought a shellfone.*

What do rhinos eat for breakfast? *Hornflakes.*

How do you make angry cookies? *With frown sugar.*

Why was the design for the new coffee mug scrapped? *The marketing team couldn't get it past the cup-board.*

Where was the world's deadliest assassin born? *The Blamazon Painforest.*

What do cows do for fun on Friday night? *They go dancing at the meatball.*

What do you call a dry piece of cake? *A Sahara Dessert.*

How do Inuit hide from closet monsters? *They seal the door shut.*

Why did the lantern fail his algebra test? *He was a bit dim.*

What did the bank machine name his kid? *Rich.*

What color firetruck did the zombie want for Christmas? *"Fright red."*

What vegetable should you never give to people who have problems swallowing? *Artichoke.*

What do bullfrogs drink when they're trying to lose weight? *Diet Croak.*

Why was the math teacher moved to the athletics department? *He changed his name to Jim.*

Why did he change his name to Jim? *He didn't like being called Jimothy.*

Made in the USA
Middletown, DE
06 April 2018